MELODY & RHYTHM PERMUTATIONS

MORE THAN 300 EXERCISES FOR MALLETS AND OTHER INSTRUMENTS
by Emil Richards

T0079955

CONTENTS

ISBN 978-1-4234-6992-6

HAL•LEONARD®
CORPORATION

7777 W. BLUEMOUND RD. P.O. BOX 13819 MILWAUKEE, WI 53213

In Australia Contact:
Hal Leonard Australia Pty. Ltd.
4 Lentara Court
Cheltenham, Victoria, 3192 Australia
Email: ausadmin@halleonard.com.au

Visit Hal Leonard Online at
www.halleonard.com

Tritones

(Pages 2–6)

Tritones divide the octave into two parts. When played in the sequential patterns at tempo, you'll be pleasantly surprised at their melodic character.

EX 1

EX 2

4

EX 17

Double Tritones

(Pages 7–9)

Double tritones are part of the double diminished scale and contain many of the upper extensions of the dominant seventh chord.

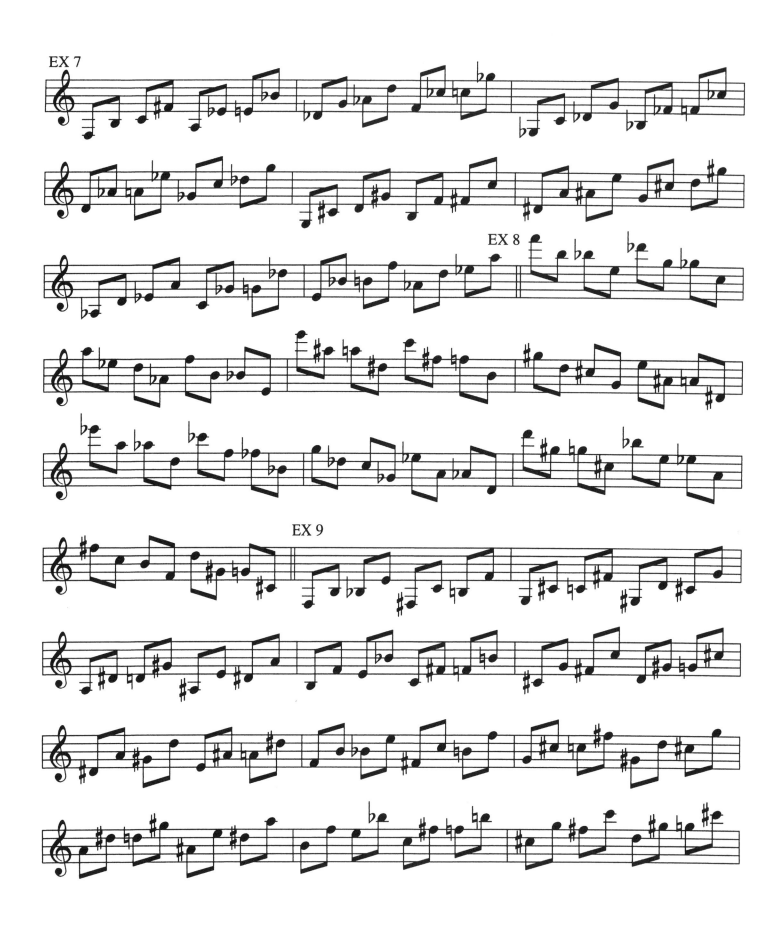

Double Diminished

(Pages 10–13)

Building on chord analysis and improvisation of the preceding section, think about the chord symbols over every two bars. Notice that each chord comprises the root, third, fifth, dominant seventh, ♭9, ♯9, +11 (♭5), and thirteenth (sixth) of its scale.

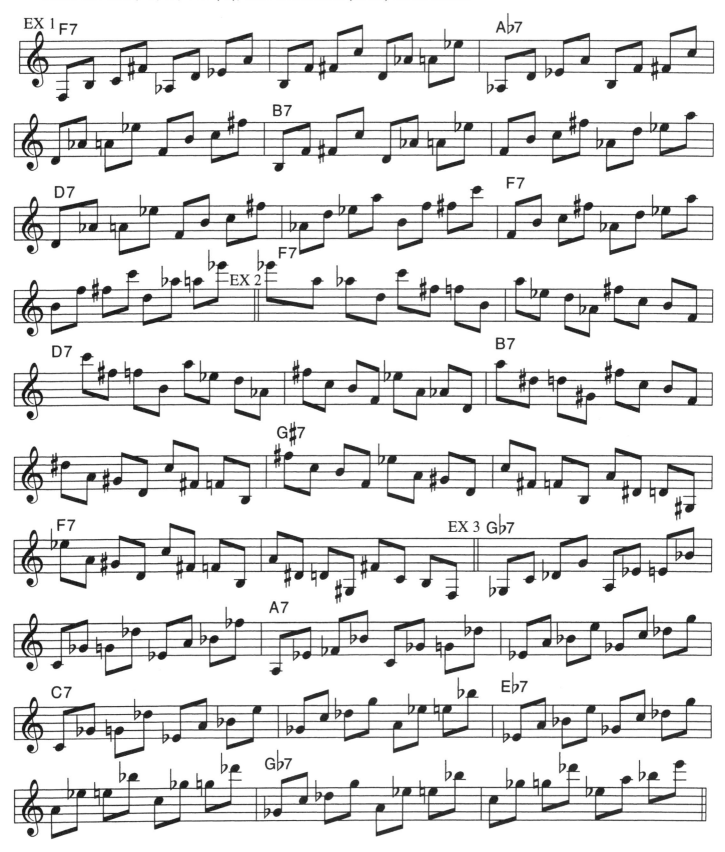

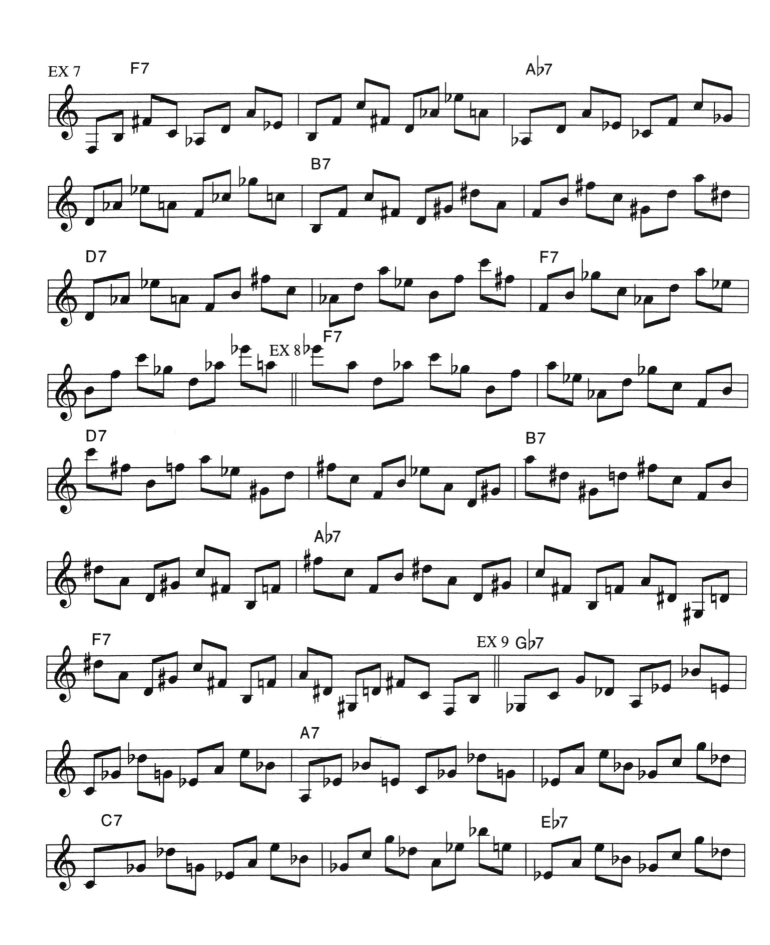

Without Looking

(Pages 14–17)

Playing octaves on mallet instruments presents challenges to your motor skills because the lower bars are larger than the upper bars. To play at faster tempi, you must be able to adjust without looking at the bars. Concentrate on looking at the music while seeing the instrument with your peripheral vision.

Thirteenth Chords

(Pages 18–20)

Mallet players can usually play only four notes simultaneously, hence four-note thirteenth chord exercises. Note how the voicing moves up in half steps, then whole steps; minor, then major thirds.

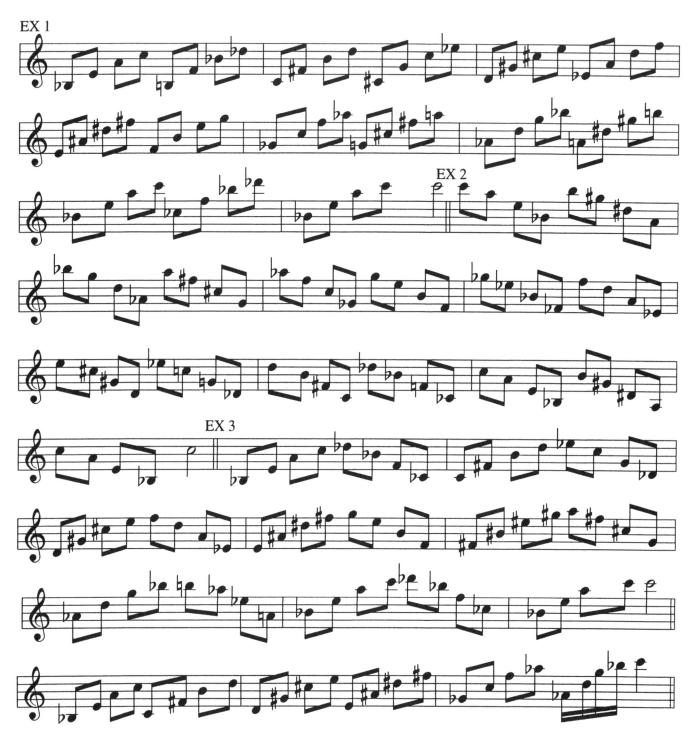

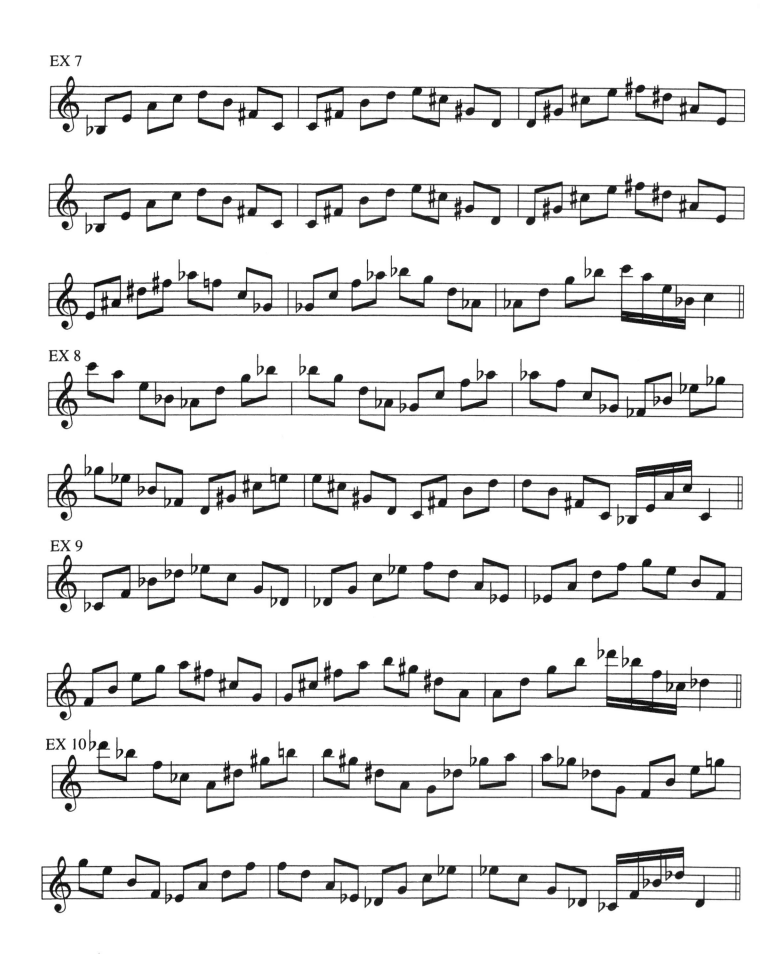

22

Thirteenth Add –9

These exercises of 13–9 chords alternately ascend, then descend in half steps. When you're comfortable playing as written, try alternate hand sticking.

Thirteenth Add 9

The same applies to the natural ninth chord added to the thirteenth. All of these exercises ascend by a minor second. Notice that by the third exercise in each series (m9, natural, and +9), you will have covered all twelve keys.

Thirteenth Add +9

The same thirteenth-chord runs apply again with the raised ninth in the chord. Try sticking with two rights, then two lefts at the beginning and end of each chord.

Thirteenths in 7/8

These thirteenth chords are grouped rhythmically 4 + 3, ascending and descending by minor seconds, major seconds, major and minor thirds, and perfect fourths. On pages 32–34, the rhythmic permutations are reversed.

Cycles in 5/4 as 3 + 2

Cycles of fourths in all their melodic and rhythmic permutations in groups of 3 + 2. This series moves from minor seconds to perfect fourths apart.

35

8va Basso 2nd X

38

EX 15

EX 16

EX 17

EX 26

Cycles of Fourths in 5/4 as 3 + 2

EX 29

45

Cycles in 5/4 as 2 + 3

Cycles of fourths in all their melodic and rhythmic permutations in groups of 2 + 3. Try alternate hands and double sticking.

EX 1

EX 2

More Cycles in 5/4

EX 11

EX 12

EX 13

57

EX 19

EX 21

Cycles of Fourths in Seven as 4 + 3

Using the Cycle of Fourths, the following pages demonstrate—through melody and rhythm—how these exercises can be permuted to play as pretty passages with a 4/8 plus 3/8 breakdown. These all move in different intervals. Try alternate or double sticking.

EX 5

EX 6

EX 7

EX 8

EX 15

EX 16

EX 19

EX 20

EX 21

EX 22

EX 26

Ex 27

EX 28

EX 29

EX 43

EX 44

EX 45

78

Ex 52

EX 54

EX 55

EX 56

EX 57

EX 58

EX 59

EX 60

EX 66

EX 67

85

EX 77

Cycles of Fourths in Seven as 3 + 4

Cycles of Fourths in all their melodic and rhythmic permutations are grouped in 3 + 4 rhythms. The intervals move in minor then major seconds, thirds, and fourths. All the exercises can be played in alternate or double sticking.

EX 1

EX 2

EX 16

EX 17

EX 18

100

EX 66

Sew Buttons on Your Ole' Man's Pants

This piece incorporates many of the permutations found in the preceding exercises. It is played [as eighth notes] 2 2 3, 2 2 3 in the first bar, and 3 3 3 3 2 in the second. This cycle plays four times. Bar nine is broken down as 5 5 4 or 2 3, 2 3, 2 2 for four bars. The last four bars rhythmically repeat the first four bars. When improvising on the changes, try to permute these numbers to equal 7 or 14.